REBUILT

Alpona Das

BookLeaf Publishing

India | USA | UK

Made with ❤ on the BookLeaf Publishing Platform
www.bookleafpub.in
www.bookleafpub.com

To the Almighty

for providing me with strength through it all.

To Mumma, Papa and Anamika

for literally everything.

To Mrs Sowmya Varadharajan

for playing a significant role in shaping me as a
literary enthusiast.

To you, dear reader,

for giving me your precious time and inspiring me
to write these verses in the first place.

Acknowledgement

This poetry collection is a culmination of journal entries, crazy fantasies, bittersweet thoughts and other messy stuff right from my high school days to my young adulting adventures, which involved the support of individuals who have and always will humble me.

First and foremost, a big thank you to my mother for inspiring me to publish my work—it all started with your encouragement—and to my father, whose support for me has been a constant source of strength.

To Anamika, my sister, for being my biggest cheerleader.

To Roosha Debnath, my editor, for patiently giving me your time to polish this book.

To Arushi Rawat, my publishing manager, for being so patient with me and giving me your precious time to clear all my queries in the publishing process.

To Mujtaba Feroz Shah, for effectively capturing my vision for this book and thereby designing the immensely beautiful cover.

To BookLeaf Publishing and its brilliant team for being with me every step of the way and helping so many aspiring authors and poets like me. Without the opportunity I received from them, this book would have remained a dream for me.

A hearty thank you to my friends and kind followers on all my socials, whose motivation gave me the courage to take this step.

And many thanks especially, to so many of you, who have chosen to spend a part of your life reading verses from this daydreamer of a girl who always hopes that her words make sense.

Preface

In the quiet aftermath of heartbreak, a void remains where love once existed. This poetry collection is born from that space—a journey through the fragments of love lost, gathering the pieces together, understanding what truly matters to you and making the bold decision to fall in love again.

Each poem reflects a step in this process—from the initial heartbreak to the slow and painful healing filled with cluttered confusions, insane trust issues and unforgiving but liberating moments of vulnerability. Writing these poems gave me the strength to look at pain objectively and made me consider it a building block to betterment. I hope that as you read, you find your reflections in these words, and probably a bit of comfort in knowing that you are not/have not been alone in your journey, and every thought that passes you in these moments is natural.

These poems are about loss, but they are also about rebuilding the love within you. May these words serve as your companion, dear reader, in your unique journey of pain and peace.

Contents

The Fleeting Marble Eyes

it was time for him
to leave immediately.
Fortune was showing me
how love is temporary.
he held my pale face
and let me know
our love was always autumn.
I locked him in an embrace
and let him know
my heart can never be wholesome.
he had no fear of tragedy
and saw no bondage of forever.
yet, I thought I saw an invisible tear
in his fleeting marble eyes,
which struck me like a knife.
I wiped the blood from me
and wiped his fading cheek.
Sweet Fortune showed me
how this so-called love was temporary.
We were out of this lyricism
and I was still committing.
He was now a phantom,
and I was still smiling.

A Dreamy Aftermath

you intruded on my dreams
becoming the fiancé so keen
as I entered the very home
which we used to call our own.
you kissed me slow
on the cheek and the brow
you were cutting fruits at the kitchen table,
I joined you there and narrated my fables.
we cooked some moments rare.
I wake up, and you aren't here.
I won't beg you to return.
I am glad how the tables turned.
If we ever see each other again,
I will smile at you as I depart,
I was in love with you, and I was insane.
But I honoured my shattered glass heart.

mornings without you

I witness the dawn every morning
when the dark blue sky turns bright orange.
it is the only way I can miss you
and the way you lit me up with your hue.
you started my day with kisses on my ears.
such a dawn in me might never again appear.

I Lost a Piece of My Heart

From the dark, tempestuous fear
to the high tide of salty tears
I lost a piece of my heart
and turned it into art.

From the peaceful, white-haired dreams
to Reality's grief-stricken screams
I lost a piece of my heart
and turned it into art.

In my head, you urge me to stay.
Through my eyes, you have nothing to say.
I lost a piece of my heart
and turned it into art.

To you, I was pretty like the high alpines.
Now you make fun of my scarred bracelet
lines.
I lost a piece of my heart
and turned it into art.

It was a bond with brittle trust
and covered with lust's stardust.
I lost a piece of my heart
and turned it into art.

I won't play the victim card shit,
it was my fault too.
I should've been more tacit.
I should've searched for no one to talk to.

Now I hear screams within, 'Oh, so late'!
'You have lost a piece of your heart!
Now is the time to retaliate
and turn your heart into furious art'!

The Last Footprint

Still breaking each day,
my heart begs me to return.
I remind it tirelessly
why it is getting those cleaves.
I stop, turn back and grab hold of its yearns,
placing a teardrop near
the last footprint I leave.

Our Secret

I won't tell them our secret.
I respect who he used to be.
I'll just tell them I tore my ankle and met
everyone's care, but where was he?

His innovative hypocrisy told them,
'She's a coward'!
even though I chose him,
a society-fearing nerd.

He never cared to know me;
pop stars know me better!
I don't know who they are,
but I knew him—the innovator.

There was no love anymore,
but hopes of being good friends
who hold a small piece of rope
at its two ends.

But the rope was just a thread,
and I pulled it too hard,
while he never tried to pull it at all.
Now they scream,
'Look at these glass heart's shards'!

His marble eyes
don't meet my brunette ones
but I won't lie,
I'm free from his conservative dungeons.

Life's a depressed dramedy
but the promise stands erect.
I respect who he used to be.
I won't tell them our secret.

Before My Private Farewell,

I hate that
they will never know what you did,
they will never know your devilish charm,
quite worse than an arrogant kid.
You're very alluring,
and you're so wretched.
Your mother is a good woman;
for her, I feel devastated.

I swear I didn't want to come here and
stretch.
But I see you every day and I still don't get
how any human can still be so filthy,
small, delusional and unhealthy.
I still get bitter and vain
when your dusted thoughts arrive.
I blame our mutual friends again,
I don't let them thrive.

I hope you know you're alone,
I hope you see it once.
I wanted to see you happy,
but you're bringing every ounce
of sadness upon you;
I hope I forgive you soon.
I will surely pray for you,
I won't scream your name at the Moon.

Before my private farewell,
I thank you for being a part of my life.
I hope you become the Sun and shine well,
I hope you are alright.
As I let you go,
I hope the shrug I gifted still fits you.
As I witness the memories' outflow,
I hope you learn to be true.

The Final Battle

Life is very musical
but sometimes, it makes us cynical.
My obsession with you is way too strong.
My conscience is trying to defeat it somehow.
The tiring battle between obsession and
conscience
fills my head with absolute dissonance.

I must win this battle.
Stalking you will lead to my destruction.
I must stop the deadly rattle
by the snake of my temptations.
I must open my door for Pain
so that you never enter again.
I must let my tears flow
so that I rebuild my heart and let you go.

the crumpled paper

she is a crumpled paper addicted to betrayal,
tired of the masks the humans wear.
nobody has ever stood up for her
while she has vehemently stopped violent
hands.

the scars from old wounds were still there
bearing no name. the prophecies of
another heartbreak should annoy her
but she is willing to let them be.
addicted to betrayal, that's what she is.

spring is coming, as well as the verdicts
of the self-imposed court judges
who will tell her she won't make it.
but the masks they wear bear her no fruit.
so, she decides to let go, as soon as
the heart shatters again, anytime soon.

From Torment to Triumph

A sudden sad thought touches me
which yells, 'I want to be free'!
I am not in despair
but I don't find myself in happy air.
I remember those
who have wronged me in all these years.
I remember those
for whom I wasted many a tear.
I remember the times
when my heart was someone's slave.
Then, I remember the times
I have been brave.

I now urge my lazy self
to stand up and march ahead
and count the number of times
she has insanely bled.
I urge her to stop giving herself
any further torment
and remember the several fragments
of sweet strength that she has showcased
and the wars that she has won unfazed.

few questions for Sadness

Are you here to heal me?
Is Happiness your enemy?
After you arrive, the tears caress my cheeks
and flood my soul gradually.
They also make my suffering louder.
What exactly are you doing here?

Happiness surely arrives when you are null
but her presence feels so ephemeral.
Your presence feels too eternal.
Are you casting a deadly spell?

How do you rule over
the kingdoms of the heart and soul?
Are you that lover of mine
who won't let me go?
I guess Time will soon reveal your identity.
Until then, can you hold my hand
and walk with me?

The Kohl-Stained Pigeon

with diamond tears,
i look in the mirror.
the kohl spreads violently
from streams of my rage leaks.

There was no love; I just rushed.
Karma's sword is out of the sheath.
It's just me who needs to hush.
It's just me who needs to breathe.

I see the dust in my hair.
The fresh joy feels unfair.
What if he also disappears
like the others, while I smile foolishly here?

I haven't loved some of them.
I was just a pigeon
feeding on validation grains
because the shattered old me
was the richest needy.

When I see reassurances written to me,
the Past Self sobs and kneels.
Currently, the dusty-haired maiden
has several wounds still bleeding.

The Teardrop

I shed a tear today
as I remembered the breathtaking day
when you held me by my waist.
Was this new love's taste?
I lost words for writing poetry
and marvelled at your artistry.

I shed the tear today
as I remembered the breathtaking day
when your hands brushed my hair.
It felt more pleasant than the summer air.
My heart built a fort
from the marble of your eyes.
My anxious attachment
arrived in love's disguise.

I shed the tear today
as I remembered the breathtaking day
when you declared your love for me.
My boundaries were blown to smithereens.
I created delusions of us
fighting the world for our love
and pushing our limits
beyond the skies above.

Then I wiped that tear today
as I remembered the heartbreaking day
when you place your hands
on my sagging shoulders
and casually announce that
our love can't get older.
I wished to die
when you had chosen to believe
the society's lies;
my bandaged heart was so naïve!

I wiped that tear today
as I remembered the heartbreaking day
when the fort was demolished
and just the breeze brushed my hair;
when new boundaries were unleashed
and I felt only the pleasant summer air.

I wiped that tear today
as I remembered the breathtaking day
when I realised you never really knew me,
and I saw the sea of tears in which you threw
me.
I knew the heart's bandage had loosened
and the dull eyes could only see a blue Sun.
You made me eat love's sharpest diamonds
then left me to bleed in peaceful silence.

rust, rain, blood

I am learning to trust again
and slowly noticing the rust on my brain,
just as you call them your friends
but they end up turning you into a fiend.
I have read this story before
and it doesn't end well.
They turn into narcissistic foes
and my flaws make my heart swell.

The tears keep flowing in thin streams
while the grief pours itself as solemn rain
I gaze at the stars and silently scream
as I struggle to break the invisible chains.
They wretchedly say, 'Your pain is nothing'!
while the blood from my wrist is still drying.
They turn my secrets into war cries,
so I make the grim choices and wipe my eyes.

Sparkles on My Scars

I used to be a covert narcissist
and a people-pleaser.
'You attract what you are'.
There are sparkles on my scars.

There was a last letter from your ex
that you had stuffed in your wallet.
Has she returned to fit your wrecks,
or you've flushed it down the toilet?

When you told me as a friend,
'My efforts are going to end',
I imagined friendships being funny,
rusted with greed and cunning.

You touched my chin
and I let you in.
You held me close
just like Jack holds Rose.

Now that we don't talk,
you take the sidewalk
at the mere sight of me.
Do you even know me?

I wonder if you meant it
when you called me, 'Dumb'!
I wonder if you cared
when you left me numb.

I wonder if your heart screams
when you don't offer me tea.
I wonder whether you would have wanted
me,
had you no fear of society.

They always find their flawed lovers
better than a flawed me.
They reveal my secrets
in immature ecstasy.
I hereby choose myself.

Now, they're firing at me and
screaming that I'm leaving.
There is blood on my luscious gown
but I'm sure I am truly breathing.

The Altar

As I arrive at the altar
willing to be sacrificed,
I gaze at Those Eyes,
and watch Them shine.
A brother leaves it all for his lover,
but also leaves his friend to die.
I am not dead; I have just gone undercover
and have arrived at the altar almost like a spy.

I just met someone new and sober
but we might not be together,
because my fragmentary heart screams
that he doesn't need me; he's too serene.
with diamond eyes and a brittle smile,
i run for days, and i run distant miles.
time tests me, i don't want to survive.
So, I arrive at the altar
wanting to be sacrificed.

But I am that simple phoenix ready to rise
after the sacrifice with silent cries,
whose poems look tired,
whose mood is bruised.
But she will face the fire
and embrace all of life's blues.

The Coronation Oath

I solemnly swear not to weep anymore
like I did when I could not walk
and everyone cared for me, except you;
like I did when you stopped looking at me
even when I placed my sword
at their throats for you;
like I did when you didn't see me at all
when I became your Past
and fought your wars for you.

I solemnly swear not to weep anymore
as I am now clean
from the dust of my prejudice
which settled ages ago
when you had broken my heart's paredes.
Now, you stare at the Sun
but don't glance at me.
I laugh and have fun
as Fate ends her party.

You turned into my tears and poems.
Your memories broke my bones.
Now, as I stand upright here,
I solemnly swear
not to add you to my folklore
and fill the sea with my tears anymore.

I solemnly swear to use these tears wisely
to water my gardens of glory,
to create diamonds for my crown,
and wipe the blood off my gown.

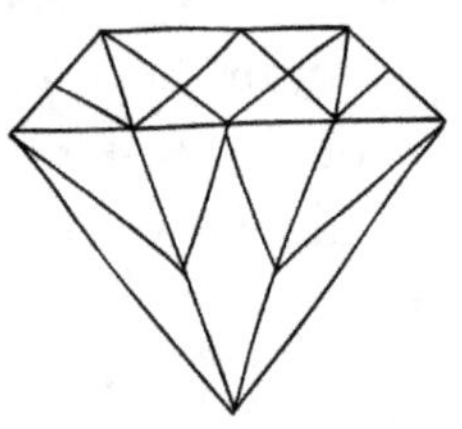

One Crown,
Many Burials

You fooled me once.
You fooled me twice.
I killed you once
and buried you several times.
I see your ghost
while raising my toast.

I rewind the scene
when no one saw your bullying.
I had no choice but to reveal this.
No one could hear my cries and pleas.
They mock even your walk now
while I just sit on the throne
with my crown on.

isolation's embrace

the last few days have treated her hard.
her choices in men
and her love life till then
made her call herself half-witted.

she reacts too much sometimes
which has made her realise
what she never knew
that she is toxic too.

she is so capable of loving,
but she has set standards based on
the green flags of her friends who are men.
well, it turns out her man-friends have
the deadliest red flags too.
what is she going to do?

she is a red flag too.
she takes everything personally.
she has been the problem many times, yes.
her attention-seeking demons within
tempt her to be eaten by them.

she speaks too much.
nonsensical curiosity gets the good of her.
she loves the roses, but she is a thorn.

she wants to be loved,
but she isn't ready at all.
trauma has gotten hold of her,
the trauma she can't figure out.

her never-ending sleepless nights
leave shadows below her eyes.
'You are the one I don't trust',
her mind tells her and sighs.

she wonders whether the rejections of love
and unnamed trauma
does these things to you.
she wonders whether the blame games
that reek of misunderstanding aimed at you
through cuss words and sugar-coated poetry
by the very people you love, do this to you.

isolation seems to be her only solace.
she does not know where to find the peace
she desperately wishes to embrace.
her trust issues are spilt all over her,
and she never even believes her odour.

she cries in the daylight
and celebrates at midnight.
hope no longer holds her hand.
time has now become the dissipating sand.
expectations don't work for her.
she is now a love-seeking wanderer.

The Old Woman's Question

a white-haired lookalike of mine asks,
'what would you do for love'?
the version of me with the childlike gaze
would have answered very likely,
'I shall destroy myself'.

bruised with betrayal's punches,
the real me is not very sure
if destruction in love
is what she craves for anymore.

she still believes somewhat that
she is willing to lie in ruins,
'But, at what cost'? she asks the ceiling.

she wonders if loving selflessly
without building the strongest fences
is something she wishes to ignore.

she wonders if she wants to chase again.
she wonders if she wants to still pretend.
she wonders if stealing his sweatshirts
make any sense at all
compared to writing him letters.

they say that love involves
accepting one's flaws.
flaws are the same as red flags, aren't they?
then I start wondering
what red and green are in the first place
when all I want are friendship and honour,
white flags and the prettiest peonies.

I sigh and finally answer to my Future Self,
'For love, I will tap my feet
and run in the wheat fields in ecstasy.

For love, I will scream at the cliff
and listen to my departing demons
echo all of them in muffled sounds.

To do all of it for love,
I don't necessarily need anyone
as love is what I breathe,
it can never destroy me'.

In the midst of it all,
I get a startling revelation
that it wasn't my love for him
that led to my destruction,
it was my bittersweet choice
and his ignored wrongdoings.

I thank the old woman
for asking me such a question.
My love has been a melody
as sweet as Mozart's.

It needs to be protected;
I have built fences of steel.
The new one shall be
allowed to hold my heart
when he lets all of his past toxicities heal.

To the One Whose Fate is Sealed with Mine,

I want you to know I'm not the easy one.
I want you to know that in love, I've won.
I want you to know that
I overthink sometimes.
I want you to know that
my heart has broken several times.

I want you to know that
I cry easily.
I want you to know that
small things make me happy.
I want you to remember
that you can cry too,
I will give you my shoulder
and be there for you.

When you embrace me
and shed every tear,
I will kiss your forehead and cheek,
and whisper poems in your ear.
I will not go to sleep
without sorting things out
provided you promise me
that you'll do the same throughout.

We will hold each other's rebuilt hearts
and kiss each other's deepest scars.
I believe in the truth, sharper than knives
and mistrust sweet words as like the honey
from the hives.

I promise to make you smile
provided you do the same each time.
I want you to be a loyal friend to me.
I want you to not be okay with shaming me.

I promise I'll be the same to you.
I want us to be equal in everything we do.
You make me humble,
and I heartily thank you
for finding the tunnel
to our fates' rendezvous.

The Old Woman's Answer

Papa asks you to smile before the camera.
You wish to be a model,
but your smile is too fake to handle.
You want to fall in love.
You want to be seen.
Yet, you don't wish to go anywhere
and leave the television screen.
You like the way your face looks.
Yet, you want to cut off your nose with twin
hooks?

You are not sure about men,
but boys around you want girls
with thin cheeks and fewer words to mumble.
Some of them want girls
because they feel lonely being single.
You can't give them what they want.
You're okay with it,
but still not okay.
You don't mind loving yourself.
You pull your cheeks!
But deep down, you want someone kind
to give you the softest kiss.

People you love do make the decisions
you're not okay with.
You stay quiet and work in tandem.
But you wish to scream at them
to let go of the mind's filth.
You turn delighted about something nice.
You do the celebratory dance all night.
You turn devastated about something
that is supposed to teach you everything.
It would help if you had hugs and peonies.
Why do you wish to be left alone completely?

When you are older,
will you have the same yearning?
Will you have the same questions within?
Will you be happy? Who knows?
You don't know, nor do they.
Whatever your future will be, little one,
never forget the many wars
that you have won.
Never give in to all those
thorns beneath the fragrant rose.
Life's races might make you a little snappy,
so, make the everyday choice of being happy.

Phantoms and Sweet Exile

Peace has never been a close friend to me
ever since those phantoms walked all over
me.
But the present feels like an eternity
when I choose not to think
about the past's enormity.

I look into your eyes
and the future knocks on my door,
but I don't open it.
I want it to storm into my home.

Patience lets me know
that peace will come and go.
The only thing that will stay
is my will to let go.

I don't know what will happen
to this glass heart rebuilt,
and I wonder what pieces are still left
to be shattered or stay still.

I guess this is what Patience wants me to see.
For now, I will let your eyes set me free.

But I am getting attached to you.
The fly is about to be captured by the sundew.
I close my eyes and
see your smile.
I see you holding my hand
in a daydream so vile.

The phantoms burn my mind's hay,
and your memory is dousing it.
I desperately want to run away,
but I see you embracing my half-wit.

The only thing looking better
than love is my quiet exile.
I can't see the future,
and the present keeps me beguiled.

The scars are building
the high walls again.
The attachment marks look like
danger signs of new pain.

I see you holding my hand
in a daydream so vile.
The only thing looking better than
love is my quiet exile.

I wasn't loved by those phantoms
in the way I should have been,
so, I don't require your presence
in the manner that I need.

My mind is sore in these winter days.
I want you, but my solace is embracing me.
I desperately want to run away,
but I see you searching for me.

The Mushroom Garden

I am certain I don't love you.
But you're the only garden I rush to:
The flashbacks are skies of a dark grey hue
and my fantasies are inedible mushrooms.

You have shown me your scars.
I don't want to forgive the ones who hurt you.
But I still don't know who you are,
the mother who birthed you,
the father who earthed you.

You're beautiful and heavenly
just like the city's longest bridge
where you took me
when life was the dullest greige.
But it is true
that I don't love you for sure,
I hope I do,
else I won't cross the bridge anymore.

I hope you love me back
and water the garden.
I hope you honour me
and paint my mushrooms golden.

Reviving the Heart's Gleam

I want you to be mine
in the unending depths of time.
Every morning, when the Sun rises,
I will look at you—where my new heart is.
I thank the Gods
for bringing you into my life.
You leave me in awe
and make my comfort thrive.
I am the CPR
that brought back my rebuilt heart's beats,
but you are the star
that makes it feel elite.

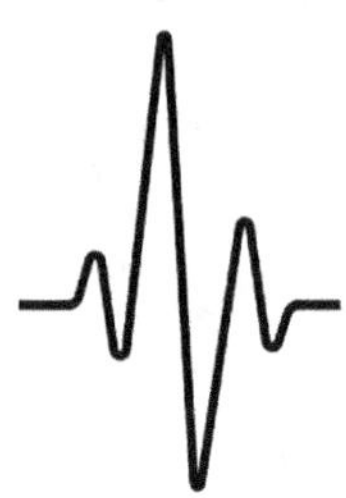

Saved by Your Light

I ask, 'Why do you want to be with me'?
You say, 'The little things you do set me free'.
I had urged you not to wait for me,
yet, you kept the lantern burning with glee.

I can't be with you all the time,
no matter how much I want you to be mine.
I see you when I lift my eyes from the screen
and let you make my soft edges shine.

I murdered the Past Me.
I don't plead guilty to this felony.
But I forgot how to survive,
you have made me thrive.

Your eyes turn my world upside down.
Your radiance lights up all the ghost towns.
You saved me from shooting myself dead,
so I have chosen to love you instead.

Venom to Vows

The snakes are everywhere.
I have just shed my skin as well.
But I am no longer venomous, I swear,
since the day I truly fell.

I can show you how much I love you,
but the scars wash me entirely
just like heavy rain.
I have been bruised in black and blue.
I overthought everything;
I counted every grain.

You tell me not to wait.
You show me the exit gate.
But I can see your eyes holding me back.
I will stay and defend Past's attacks.

God wishes to give me a lesson.
I think I have been summoned.
If our red string breaks under fate's tension,
my tears shall be shimmering diamonds.

Your lips on my forehead feel so true.
You've told me you like peonies too.
Hold my hand, my love, I won't let you go.
Take your time, my love, let's take it slow.

Whispers of Insecurity

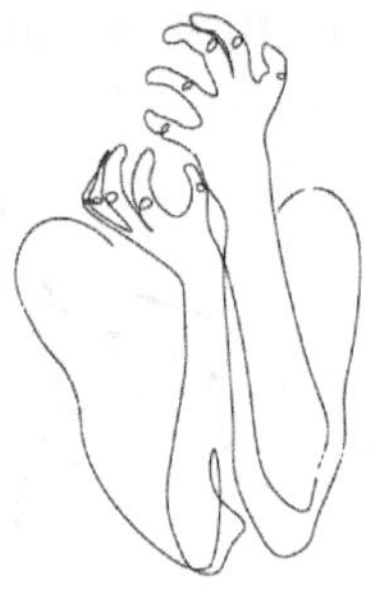

I swear I love you,
but I have doubts too.
I'm blinded by insecurities.
My mind's in disharmony.

You don't share some anecdotes with me.
You always change the topic so subtly.
I am sorry, I can't help it.
I have been killed several times in minutes.

The phantoms still love their former lovers
so my suspicions are always ushered.
I hope you forgive me for all this.
I hope you still don't think about your ex.

I sincerely hope you remember
that I have been bruised in black and blue.
Forgive me, and I will surrender,
and let my eyes heal by your love's hue.

I don't like Valentine's Day.

I yearn for a lot more
but the spring chills turn my mind sore.
They all celebrate a single day
for love and get so carried away.

But I wish for an eternity
with your arms around me
as we laugh and make love,
then gaze at the skies above.

Can you see my red cheeks?
I am yearning for your soft kiss
on my cold hands scarred
from the past's burn marks.

When Summer arrives
after this so-called love's day,
caress my faded maroon hair while
we see the Milky Way.

My new heart does not need
just one day to beat.
The past love I licked off knives

shan't make me retreat.
Take me to places away
from this ghost town within me
as I celebrate you not for a single day,
but a perpetuity.

From Tears to Toasts

Were you scared that you might not have me
or was it extreme ecstasy?
Remember when I was crying in your car
and you didn't take me to the bar?
You took me to the gardens instead
and I thanked God for our heavenly tread.

I swear I have loved you in all these years.
Your reflection is there in all my tears.
Fixated on my eyes is your pink-lipped smile.
I wish to cry while missing you,
but Patience keeps trying.

The mountain to your heart has been
a dangerously steep ascent.
But I have successfully climbed to its peak
and received your consent.

It is time to raise the toast to you
as I commence our wedding speech.
Let us welcome our fates' rendezvous
and build promises to keep.

Paradise Across the Room

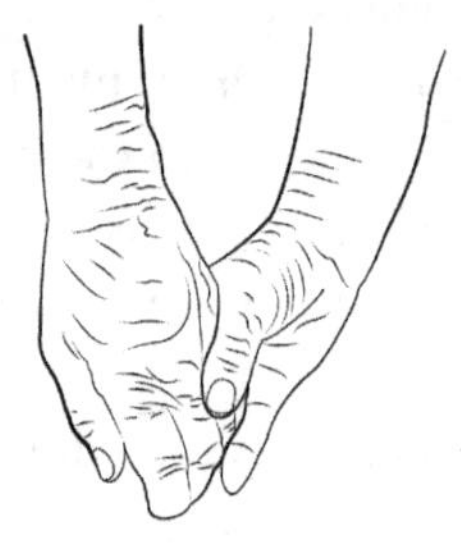

You're sitting with your kin.
Across from you,
I'm sitting with mine.
After every giggle,
we lock eyes.
Our smiles are warm.
Our love resembles paradise.
Then we look away again,
valuing our lives with grace.
Dear Cupid smiles at us
for honouring each other's space.

9 789363 302495